T0145052

# Dream Of

Written by Gabriella Mesiha

Illustrated by Kiran Vashisht

WestBow Press books may be ordered through booksellers or by contacting:

WestBow Press
A Division of Thomas Nelson & Zondervan
1663 Liberty Drive
Bloomington, IN 47403
www.westbowpress.com
844-714-3454

Interior Image Credit: Kiran Vashisht

Scripture quotations are taken from the Complete Jewish Bible by David H. Stern. Copyright © 1998. All rights reserved. Used by permission of Messianic Jewish Publishers.

ISBN: 979-8-3850-0606-9 (sc)
ISBN: 979-8-3850-0607-6 (hc)
ISBN: 979-8-3850-0609-0 (e)

Library of Congress Control Number: 2023916351

Print information available on the last page.

WestBow Press rev. date: 12/15/2023

WESTBOW
PRESS®
A DIVISION OF THOMAS NELSON
& ZONDERVAN

To my 4 little Arrows, my perfect gifts
from the Father of heavenly lights.

## This book belongs to:

_____

Dream of a delightful tea party with sprinkle covered cupcakes, eating all that you can.

My divine little one, always remember you are the child of the Great I AM.

Dream of playing at the park, with butterflies tickling your tummy as you fly high on the swings.

You are the precious child of Elohim and He protects you under the shadow of His Wings.

Dream of all the different kind of animals you would see at the zoo.

God is faithful, merciful and compassionate, dear child this is true.

Dream of wearing your favourite gumboots and splashing in puddles on a rainy day.
You fill my heart with such joy, may Adonai favour you always this I pray.

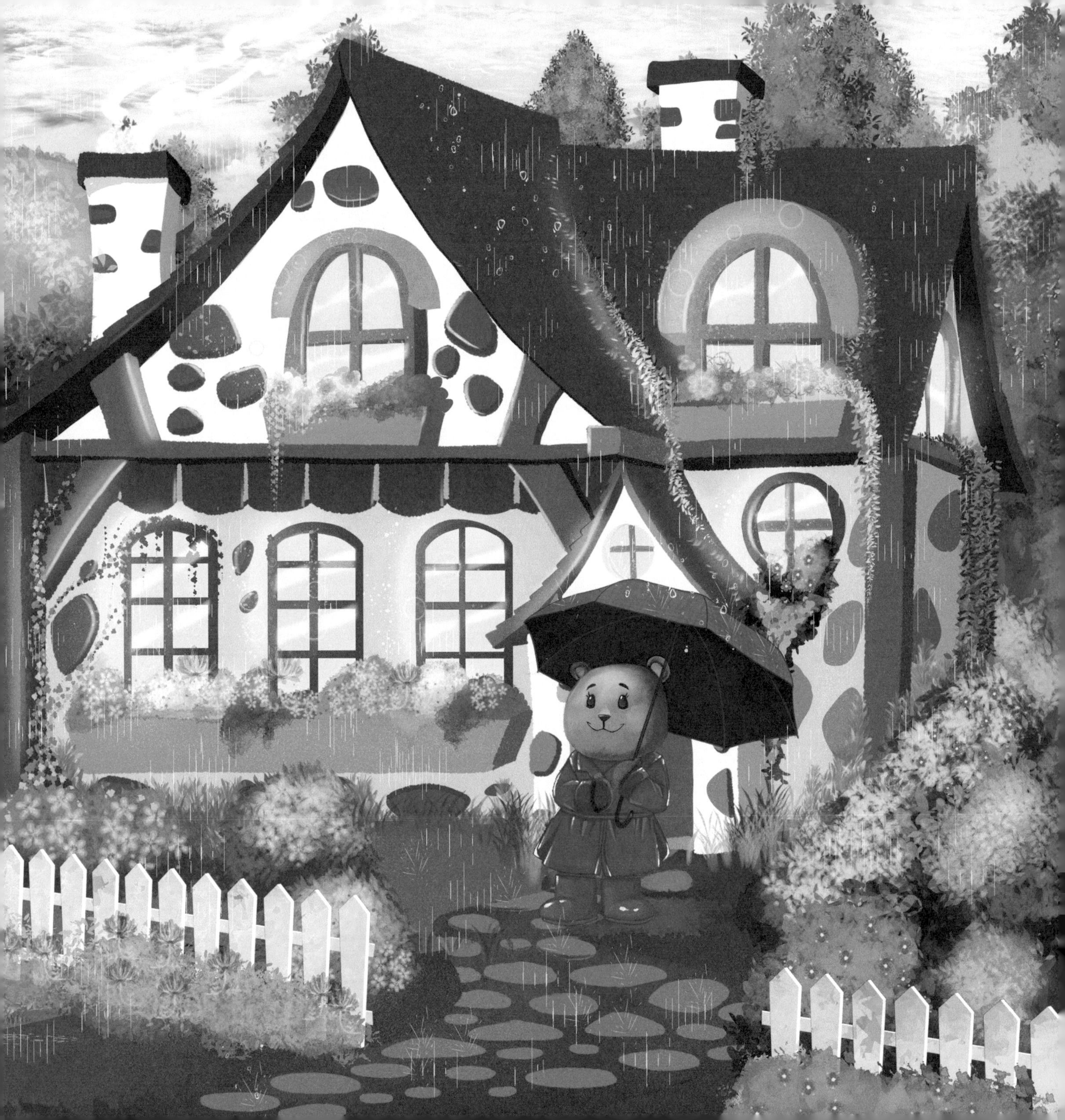

Dream of running through a field of flowers in full bloom, down a winding path.

My little precious one, I love your warm snuggly cuddles and your cute unique laugh.

Dream of splashing in the waves and building sandcastles at the beach.

My clever child, keep your heart believing
and all your goals you shall reach.

Dream of building a super cool racetrack
and having the fastest car.
   Trust in El Shaddai, follow His commands
and my child you will go far.

Dream of creating something special with buttons, sparkles, pom poms and glue.

Your family and friends love you dearly, and your Heavenly Father does too.

Dream of your guardian angel
watching over you as you
close your eyes to rest.

Remember always you are
a royal child of YAHWEH,
and you are truly blessed.

Dream of rainbows, rubies,
diamonds and our
Bright Morning Star.
Sleep peacefully
my treasure,
the Dear Lord
loves you,
just
the
way
YOU
are.

This book was inspired by a rhyme I made whilst putting my children to bed one night. The rhyme was so popular with my children that it became a part of our nightly bedtime routine. I say this rhyme to them each night as I tuck them in, then they recite the rhyme back to me. The original rhyme I made is very similar to the one in the last page in this book.

The rhyme came about one bedtime when my eldest child (4 at the time) asked me, "Mamma, what is heaven like?". I couldn't think specifically of a scripture being asked on the spot (as children usually do), but from memory I recalled reading scriptures describing heaven as full of wonderful colours and precious gems. And that is how the rhyme unfolded.

I felt so blessed by the joy this rhyme had brought to my children that I felt inspired to write a children's bedtime rhyme book to acknowledge it. I have been filled with so much joy writing this book and collaborating with the illustrator for the artwork, it has truly been a project of love.

One night during my bible studies, I came across the scripture that was so closely related to the initial rhyme I had made located in Revelations in my bible:

(The Complete Jewish Study Bible, 2016, Revelations 4:3)

The One sitting there gleamed like diamonds and rubies, and a rainbow shining like emerald encircled the throne.

I hope you and your family are filled with comfort and joy through reading this precious bedtime rhyme book.

May God Bless you and shine His face on you,

Gabriella Mesiha

Printed in the United States
by Baker & Taylor Publisher Services